healthy juices
for healthy kids

OVER 70 JUICE AND SMOOTHIE RECIPES FOR KIDS OF ALL AGES

WENDY SWEETSER

healthy juices
for healthy kids

OVER 70 JUICE AND SMOOTHIE RECIPES FOR KIDS OF ALL AGES

First published in 2010 by New Holland Publishers (UK) Ltd
London • Cape Town • Sydney • Auckland

Garfield House
86–88 Edgware Road
London W2 2EA
United Kingdom
www.newhollandpublishers.com

80 McKenzie Street
Cape Town 8001
South Africa

Unit 1, 66 Gibbes Street
Chatwood
NSW 2067
Australia

218 Lake Road
Northcote
Auckland
New Zealand

ISBN 978 1 84773 612 3

Senior Editor: Corinne Masciocchi
Designer: Lucy Parissi
Photographer: Ian Garlick
Home economy and food styling: Wendy Sweetser
Production: Laurence Poos
Editorial Direction: Rosemary Wilkinson

2 4 6 8 10 9 7 5 3 1

Reproduction by Pica Digital PTE Ltd, Singapore
Printed and bound by Tien Wah Press (PTE) Ltd, Singapore

contents

'Please Mum, I'm thirsty, can I have a drink?' is a cry mothers are all too familiar with and it's true that children do need plenty of liquids to stop them becoming dehydrated. Due to their low body weight, children are more vulnerable than adults to the effects of dehydration and this can cause not just tiredness, headaches and mood swings but make it difficult for them to concentrate too. It can also prevent the digestive system from working efficiently as bowels need plenty of fluid to avoid constipation.

KEEPING YOUR KIDS HEALTHY

Fresh juices and smoothies contain lots of nutrients to help keep children healthy and are a useful way of ensuring that picky eaters, who normally turn their noses up at fruit and vegetables, add to their recommended daily allowance.

Fruit and vegetable juices are an excellent source of vitamins, particularly vitamin C. This valuable vitamin helps children absorb iron from their food and build up their immune systems to protect them against bacteria and viruses. The recommended daily allowances of vitamin C vary slightly from country to country but the following can be taken as a guide:

* 25 mg for 4 to 8 year olds
* 45 mg for 9 to 13 year olds
* For 14 to 18 year olds, 75 mg is the recommended daily allowance for boys and 65 mg for girls.

The recommended daily allowances for adults are 75 mg for women and 90 mg for men. As a 250-ml (9 fl-oz) glass of freshly squeezed orange juice contains around 120 mg of vitamin C, it's easy to see just how valuable a contribution a juice can make to a healthy, balanced diet.

Smoothies, where fruit or vegetables are puréed with milk or yoghurt, can also play an important part in keeping your kids healthy. Milk, the ultimate superfood, is packed with a range of nutrients including calcium, protein, zinc, iodine and vitamins A and B and, as whole fruit are used to make smoothies, the resulting drinks also contain dietary fibre. Calcium is essential for strong teeth and bones, whilst protein repairs body tissues like muscles and zinc boosts the immune system. Iodine is needed to help the body convert food to energy, vitamin A is important for good eyesight, vitamin B for healthy growth, and dietary fibre keeps the body regular.

Yoghurt is low in fat, high in calcium and good for the digestive tract but it's best to opt for natural yoghurt that contains probiotic bacteria and sweeten it yourself with a little honey, if necessary, rather than buy a flavoured yoghurt that can contain large amounts of sugar or artificial sweeteners. Although skimmed milk should not be given to children under five years old, after that age low-fat yoghurt and skimmed or semi-skimmed milk can be used to make drinks.

When sweetening juices, honey is a better choice than sugar as honey increases the level of protective antioxidants in the blood and softens sharper juices with its own warm, rounded flavour. Maple syrup is another natural sweetener that, amongst a range of health benefits, contains zinc and manganese to help the immune system.

What are the best drinks for children?
Whilst persuading children to have a drink is rarely a problem, the difficult part can be steering them away from heavily sweetened

7

juice drinks, squashes and fizzy pop in favour of a healthier option. Children have a naturally sweet tooth and many consume too much sugar from fizzy drinks that are high in additives and low in nutrients and can lead to a variety of problems such as hyperactivity, weight gain and tooth decay. A single can of ordinary cola contains an eye-watering 10 teaspoons of sugar, so as well as being nutritionally poor value, it's high in calories too.

The two healthiest drinks for kids are without question plain water and milk, and all children should be encouraged to consume plenty of both. But, like adults, children thrive on variety so including healthy options such as homemade fruit juices and smoothies will not only add interest to what they drink but increase the amount of fresh fruit and vegetables in their diet.

Can my children get all their recommended daily portions of fruit and vegetables from juices and smoothies?
When juice is extracted from a fruit or vegetable, the fibre content is greatly reduced so the nutritional benefit is less than if you were to eat the whole fruit. For this reason a 150 ml (¼ pt) glass of juice counts as only one of the five recommended daily portions, however many different kinds of fruit and vegetables are used to make it. Juice can also only count as one portion a day, regardless of how many glasses are drunk, as the nutritional benefits from juice are lower than those from whole fruit and vegetables. It must also be 100% pure juice or juice from concentrate, as squashes and 'juice drinks' contain added water and sugar so cannot be counted.

Smoothies, on the other hand, are made by crushing whole fruit or vegetables with juice, so they contain higher levels of carbohydrate, fibre, energy, sugars and vitamin C than pure juices. A 250 ml (9 fl oz) glass of smoothie made with 150 ml (¼ pt) fruit juice and 80 g (3 oz) fruit is equal to two portions of the RDA.

Can I only use fresh fruit to make juices?
Frozen, canned, bottled and reconstituted dried fruit, as well as fresh, can all be used, enabling you to make a wide variety of juices even when your kids' favourite fruits are out of season. When making drinks using canned or bottled fruit, choose those canned in fruit juice rather than syrup to avoid the extra sugar. The juice from the can or bottle can also be added to the drink for extra flavour.

Which vegetables are most suitable for juices?

Naturally sweet vegetables that are popular with children, such as carrots and cucumber, are particularly good, as are other vegetables like spinach and beetroot that are not usually junior crowd-pleasers. Juicing vegetables with fruit not only helps mask their flavour – beetroot in particular can taste rather earthy on its own – it can also produce spectacularly coloured drinks, such as bright orange when carrots are added or a rich purple with beetroot.

I prefer not to add sugar to my kids' drinks but will they complain they're not sweet enough?

Although individual tastes vary, the juice recipes in this book should be sweet enough without the necessity to add extra sugar. All fruit and vegetable juices, whether they're ones you've made yourself or bought ready made, tend to be sweeter than the individual ingredients used to make them as natural sugars in the fruit and vegetables become concentrated when their juice is extracted.

Some fruits such as pears, mangoes and strawberries are naturally very sweet so, when using these to make a drink, it's worth combining them with sharper flavours such as citrus fruits to ensure a good balance. Taste the finished juice and if you feel your children will complain that it's too sharp, add a little runny honey or maple syrup to sweeten it if necessary. Alternatively, you can just change the balance of ingredients in a recipe by cutting down the quantity of citrus or leaving it out altogether. If you do add honey or maple syrup to a juice, it's important to do this just before serving as the longer a juice is left to stand the more its flavours – including its natural sweetness – will develop.

Older children and teenagers are likely to have more sophisticated palates than their younger siblings so a particularly sweet juice may need sharpening with the addition of a squeeze of fresh lemon or lime juice to suit their taste.

Are juices suitable for children of all ages?
The recipes in this book are aimed at children aged between four and 16 years old, although hopefully they will appeal to the grown-up members of the family just as much. It is recommended that juices should not be given to babies under six months old and the amount of juice given to young children should always be carefully monitored to avoid them filling themselves

up with smoothies and fresh fruit drinks and leaving no room for lunch or supper!

Although good for kids – juices contain valuable minerals and vitamins, and milk or yoghurt-based smoothies contain calcium – most of the calories in fruit juices come from sugars and carbohydrates rather than protein or fat, so over-indulgence risks a child's diet becoming unbalanced. The sugar and acid in fruit juices can also damage tooth enamel if large quantities are drunk between meals. For this reason it's a good idea to dilute juices with water for younger children and make sure they brush their teeth before bedtime.

What equipment do I need to make juices and smoothies?

There's no need to buy a special juice extractor as all the recipes in this book can be made using either a liquidizer or food processor. However, if you do own a juice extractor, this can be used to make the orange, apple, pineapple, grapefruit and other juices that are blended with the whole fruit and vegetables in the recipes, rather than buying ready made ones.

Citrus fruit juices can be made using a simple old-fashioned lemon squeezer or manual press but if you do put oranges and grapefruit through a juice extractor cut away the outer layer of rind first using a sharp knife, peeler or zester, as it will give the drink a bitter taste if left on. The pith doesn't need removing as it contains valuable nutrients and won't taint the flavour of the juice.

When putting fruit or vegetables through a juice extractor, it's not necessary to peel them first or remove cores and pips, unless

introduction

the skin, stalks or stones are very coarse and hard. As many of the nutrients found in fruit and vegetables are just under the skin, the resulting juices will be healthier. However, all produce, whether organic or non-organic, must first be washed thoroughly in running water.

When using a liquidizer or food processor, fruit and vegetables need to be peeled first and the pips, cores, seeds and stalks removed. It is particularly important to remove the seeds from tomatoes, as well as the skin, as if these are blitzed with the rest of the pulp, they will give the juice a bitter taste.

When whole fruit and vegetables are blended with juice, milk or yoghurt in a liquidizer or food processor, the resulting drinks are thicker than those made using a juice extractor. Some very pulpy ones will also thicken up on standing so might need letting down with water, milk or extra fruit or vegetable juice to dilute the drink to the desired consistency.

Do I need to strain juices before serving?
This is very much down to personal taste. Although pips and stones can be removed from most fruits, it's not possible to do this with soft fruits such as raspberries and blackberries. If your kids don't like drinks 'with bits in', strain juices containing these fruits before pouring them into glasses or simmer the fruit first with a little water or fruit juice until it becomes pulpy and can be pushed through a sieve to remove the seeds.

Similarly, whilst it's easy to skin peaches, plums and tomatoes, it's not practical with small fruits like cherries, grapes and blueberries. When blended, the skins of these fruits won't break down completely but will remain in the juice as finely chopped flecks so, once again, strain the juice before drinking if preferred.

Should I only make juices from fruit and vegetables that are ripe and blemish-free?

Don't buy produce that's past its best as the nutrient levels and juice content of fruit and vegetables diminishes with age. They need to be ripe, as they will have a greater concentration of antioxidants, but still firm and fruit should smell fragrant and sweet.

If you grow your own fruit and freeze the excess to use throughout the year, freeze it as soon as you can after picking to preserve as many of the nutrients as possible.

How far ahead can I make juices?

Most juices and smoothies are best drunk freshly made as the longer they're kept the more vitamins they lose. Once exposed to the air, juices begin to oxidise and those containing apples and bananas can discolour and start to turn brown. Citrus flavours also become more pronounced and dominate other, more delicate, fruits.

However, although it's a good idea to give kids a juice or smoothie at breakfast time since they contain so many valuable nutrients, most weekday mornings in family homes are rushed affairs with everyone late for school or work. If preparing a fresh juice is one job too many, it's fine to make it the night before and keep the juice in a covered container in the fridge. If a juice left to stand has separated, give it a good stir up before pouring into glasses.

Some juices have an awful lot of froth. How can I get rid of this as my kids don't like it?

Some fruits, such as apples and pears, are notorious for producing juices with thick, frothy heads and the simplest way to remove or reduce this is by skimming it off with a spoon or by spraying the froth with a fine mist of cold water to help it settle.

If you have a juice extractor, this will probably have been supplied with a juice-collecting jug complete with a built-in froth separator that acts as a lid and will do the job for you. This specially designed lid traps the froth in the jug as the juice is poured out. Alternatively, you can simply serve a frothy drink with a straw so the juice is sucked from the bottom of the glass, leaving the froth behind.

13

14

Are there any other special juicing tips I should know?

With fruits that contain lots of juice, such as oranges or grapefruit, it's a good idea to prepare them on a plate – or straight over the bowl of a food processor or liquidizer goblet – so any juice that drips out isn't lost.

When liquidizing whole fruit with juice, milk or yoghurt, a smooth mixture is easier to obtain if you add the liquid in several batches to the liquidizer or food processor. Pulse the mixture in small bursts after each addition, stopping to push any pulp down the sides of the bowl as necessary.

My kids love ice lollies, crushes and slushies. Are there any special tips for making these?

When making ice lollies from fruit juice, it's worth remembering that as the juice freezes it will expand so don't fill the moulds quite to the top. The lollies then need to be left in the freezer until they are still just soft enough for the sticks to be pushed in but sufficiently solid to prevent the sticks floating to the surface.

As the flavour and sweetness of fruit diminishes when it's frozen, ice lollies made with subtly flavoured fruits benefit from being sweetened with a little honey.

Full-flavoured fruits such as mangoes, oranges or summer berries are fine on their own but add honey if they are blended with unsweetened natural yoghurt or fromage frais to counteract any tartness.

To remove frozen lollies that are sticking stubbornly to their moulds, dip each mould in a bowl of hot water for a few seconds to loosen the lollies sufficiently for them to be lifted out. Avoid tugging on the lolly stick as you could pull this out and leave the lolly behind!

If you have an ice cream or sorbet machine, this can be used to make crushes. It also means you don't have to keep an eye on the half-frozen mixture and remove it from the freezer to break up ice crystals.

Whilst slushies can be made using either a food processor or liquidizer, those made in a food processor will have a stronger flavour as the fruit needs little or no liquid added to it to reduce it to pulp, whereas liquid is needed to crush fruit in a liquidizer. The recipes for slushies in this book include the quantities of liquid required to do that but if using a food processor the liquid can be reduced to a couple of tablespoonfuls or omitted altogether.

Our family diet doesn't include dairy products, what can I use instead of milk and yoghurt?
Soya milk and yoghurt can replace cow's milk and yoghurt in the recipes. As soya is enriched with calcium and is high in isoflavones, the antioxidants believed to protect the walls of arteries from potential damage caused by harmful chemicals called free radicals, it makes a healthy alternative to dairy products.

Can children have juices before bedtime?
It's best to give children milky drinks directly before bedtime and to avoid any juice with a high acid content as this can soften their tooth enamel. As the acid in a fruit juice remains on the teeth for about half an hour to an hour before it disperses, any brushing during this time could cause permanent damage to a child's teeth.

Most of the recipes in the Bedtime Soothers (pages 142–59) chapter of this book are milk based or contain only a small amount of fruit juice. The Blackberry, apple and plum cordial (page 151) and Lemon kiss (page 150) recipes, which contain a higher proportion of fruit, are designed to be drunk slightly earlier in the evening – ideally an hour or so before bedtime when you're settling the kids down for some quiet time – so any acid can disperse before they brush their teeth.

ABOUT THE RECIPES

Juices and smoothies aren't just good for your kids, they're fun to make as well, so get them involved in helping you try out the recipes in this book and then encourage them to start creating their own.

The quantities given for each recipe are approximate and will vary according to the size of fruit and vegetables used and how much juice or pulp they contain.

The thickness of drinks will depend on how large fruit and vegetables are and how much pulp they make, and if you are adding yoghurt, the type used. How thick your kids like their drinks is also down to personal preference so dilute them with extra juice, water or milk as required.

15

16   breakfast juices and smoothies

Grapes come in many colours and sizes, from tiny, sour berries with thick black skins, to luscious, green muscat fruit with their honeyed flavour and elderflower aroma. Although red grapes have higher levels of antioxidants than the green variety, all grapes contribute a useful amount of vitamin A to our diet – important for good eyesight, growth, healthy tissues and strong bones. This juice is very frothy so leave it to settle for a few minutes before pouring into glasses, or use a straining jug to trap the froth as you pour.

18   pineapple, peach and grape flip

Makes 400 ml (14 fl oz)

2 pineapple rings, fresh or canned in fruit juice

1 peach

300 ml (½ pt) red grape juice

If using fresh pineapple, cut away the skin, dig out the brown 'eyes' with the point of a sharp knife and remove the tough centre core. Chop the flesh into small pieces. Put the peach in a heatproof bowl, cover with boiling water and leave for 1 minute. Drain, cool the peach under cold water and cut into quarters. Remove the stone and peel away the skin. Put the pineapple, peach and grape juice in a liquidizer and blend until smooth. Pour into glasses and serve.

Our grandmothers used to tell us that if we ate up our carrots we'd be able to see in the dark and it's true that one large carrot contains enough beta-carotene for our bodies to convert into a whole day's dose of vitamin A – essential for bright, healthy eyes. Most children love carrots for their sweet flavour and carrot juice is a useful way of adding extra nutrients to junior drinks. If the juice is too thick, let it down with water or fruit juice from the canned apricots, if using.

20   school's out

Makes 600 ml (1 pt)

3 fresh apricots or
6 apricot halves
canned in fruit juice

1 apple

300 ml (½ pt)
carrot juice

If using fresh apricots and you prefer to peel them, put in a heatproof bowl, cover with boiling water and leave for 1 minute. Drain, cool the apricots under cold water and cut in half. Remove the stones and peel away the skin. If leaving unpeeled, simply halve and remove the stones. Core the apple, peel and cut into quarters. Place in a liquidizer with the apricots, add the carrot juice and blend until smooth. Pour into glasses and serve.

Ripe, plump tomatoes – vegetables that are really fruits – are major players in a healthy diet and the good news for kids is that eating them as ketchup, as a spaghetti sauce or in a juice is just as beneficial as tackling them in one of mum's leafy salads. Rich in antioxidants like vitamin C, flavonoids and the carotenoid, lycopene, tomatoes can help protect against heart disease and some cancers. Homemade tomato juice is not as concentrated, nor as red and thick, as bought juice so making your own produces a more refreshing drink.

22   simply red

Makes 600 ml (1 pt)

1 red pepper
300 g (10½ oz) ripe tomatoes
300 ml (½ pt) carrot juice

Line the grill with foil and grill the pepper until the skin blisters but isn't too blackened, turning regularly. Wrap the foil around the pepper and set aside until cold. Remove the foil, strip off the skin, halve and discard the stalk and seeds. Cut into chunks. Place the tomatoes in a heatproof bowl, pour over boiling water to cover and leave for 30 seconds. Drain, cool under cold water and quarter. Discard the skin and pips, and put the flesh in a liquidizer with the pepper and carrot juice. Blitz until smooth, pour into glasses and serve. The drink thickens on standing so if made ahead, let it down to the desired consistency with water before serving.

When strawberries are out of season make this with frozen fruit as the resulting juice will have more natural sweetness than if hard, artificially ripened berries flown in from the other side of the world are used. Strawberries, which are the only fruit to have their seeds on the outside, contain high levels of vitamin C and soluble fibre that helps break down 'bad' cholesterol in the body. If pink grapefruit juice is unavailable, ordinary grapefruit juice can be substituted.

24 breakfast blush

Makes 600 ml (1 pt)

175 g (6 oz)
strawberries

1 apple

200 ml (7 fl oz) pink
grapefruit juice

Hull the strawberries and cut any large fruit into two or three pieces. If using frozen strawberries, don't bother to defrost them first; add them to the liquidizer whilst still frozen so you have a deliciously chilled drink. Cut the apple into quarters, peel and remove the core. Put the strawberries, apple and grapefruit juice in a liquidizer and reduce to a smooth purée. Pour into glasses and serve.

Smooth nectarines are closely related to their fuzzy-skinned cousins, peaches. The only difference – apart from the skin – is that nectarines have a stronger, sweeter aroma and juicier flesh. Nectarines contain only a modest amount of vitamin C but as the other ingredients in this juice are orange and fibre-rich pineapple, your kids won't go short on their daily quota of nutrients.

26 happy mondays

Makes 500 ml (18 fl oz)

1 large orange
1 nectarine
300 ml (½ pt) pineapple juice

Cut the peel and pith away from the orange and divide the flesh into segments. Peel the nectarine by putting the fruit in a heatproof bowl and covering with boiling water. Leave to stand for 1 minute, then drain and cool the nectarine under cold water. Cut it into quarters, remove the stone and peel away the skin. If preferred, just remove the stone and leave the nectarine unpeeled. Put the orange segments, nectarine and pineapple juice in a liquidizer and blend until smooth. Pour into glasses and serve.

Ask any group of kids to name their favourite fruit and the chances are most of them will shout 'banana'. One of nature's superfoods, children love bananas as they are easy to eat and contain plenty of natural sugar to make them appealing to young palates. On the nutrients side, bananas are a great source of potassium, helping to keep blood pressure low; and eaten for breakfast, whether on their own or in a juice, they provide a sustained burst of energy and boost brain power to keep your kids going through their morning lessons.

28   kick start

Makes 600 ml (1 pt)

1 banana
150 g (5½ oz)
strawberries
300 ml (½ pt)
apple juice

Peel the banana and cut it into three or four pieces. Hull the strawberries and halve any large ones. Put the banana, strawberries and apple juice in a liquidizer and purée until smooth. Skim off the excess froth, if desired, then pour into glasses and serve.

breakfast juices and smoothies

The stones in fresh cherries can be fiddly and time-consuming to remove if you don't have a special pitting tool, so make your busy life easier by buying stoned fruit that has been canned or bottled in juice. Cherries are a useful source of fibre and both vitamins A and C, and children love their naturally sweet flavour. Any variety and colour of fresh dessert cherry is suitable so use whatever is available.

30 cherry, banana and buttermilk smoothie

Makes 700 ml (1¼ pt)

200 g (7 oz) fresh dessert cherries, pitted, or 175 g (6 oz) canned or bottled sweet cherries in fruit juice, drained weight

1 banana

150 ml (¼ pt) milk

300 ml (½ pt) buttermilk

Extra fresh cherries, to serve

Put the cherries in a liquidizer. Peel the banana, cut it into three or four pieces and add to the liquidizer with the milk and buttermilk. Blend until smooth and pour into glasses. Serve with extra fresh cherries, if liked.

This gorgeously creamy smoothie is a great way to kick-start any kid's day. Naturally sweet, bananas become even sweeter as they ripen and the starch in them turns to natural fruit sugar, so it's also perfect for using up any brown-speckled bananas left in the fruit bowl that fussy junior palates don't fancy. Wheatgerm (the fine grains left behind when white flour is milled) is rich in vitamins B and E, so adds extra nutrients to the drink.

banana, apricot and yoghurt blast

Makes 600 ml (1 pt)

1 small banana
4 apricots
200 ml (7 fl oz) milk
150 g (5½ oz) natural yoghurt
2 tsp wheatgerm

Peel the banana and cut it into three or four pieces. Halve the apricots and remove the stones. If fresh, the apricots can be skinned if wished, as per instructions on page 20. Put the banana, apricot halves, milk and yoghurt in a liquidizer and blend until smooth. Pour into glasses, sprinkle over the wheatgerm and serve.

Blueberries might look innocuous but these little berries with their dull purple skins should be included as a regular part of everyone's diet. One of nature's most powerful health foods, blueberries protect the body's cells by helping them neutralize dangerous free radicals and they also act as a natural tonic for blood vessels. Another plus guaranteed to appeal to mums and dads – even if it's lost on the younger members of the family – is blueberries' ability to help slow down the ageing process.

34 big berry delight

Makes 800 ml (1 pt 8 fl oz)

175 g (6 oz) blueberries

175 g (6 oz) strawberries

300 ml (½ pt) apple juice

3 Tbsp natural yoghurt

Extra berries, to serve

Remove any stalks from the blueberries and place in a liquidizer. Hull the strawberries, cut any large ones into halves or quarters and add to the liquidizer with the apple juice and yoghurt. Blend until smooth, then pour into glasses and serve with extra berries if wished.

Yoghurt has been made in different forms since the dawn of time. The ancient North African Bedouins were one of the first migratory tribes to discover that when milk fermented in their goatskin saddlebags, due to a combination of movement, exposure to the baking desert sun and more than a few friendly bacteria, the resulting thick mix not only kept for days but was remarkably satisfying to eat. An excellent source of calcium, look for live or bio yoghurts that keep the digestive system healthy and fight any 'bad' bugs that can creep in and cause food poisoning.

36   wake-up smoothie

Makes 600 ml (1 pt)

175 g (6 oz) strawberries

1 banana

150 g (5½ oz) vanilla yoghurt

200 ml (7 fl oz) milk

Extra strawberries, to serve

Hull the strawberries and cut any large ones into halves or quarters. Peel the banana and cut into three or four pieces. Put the strawberries, banana, yoghurt and milk in a liquidizer and blend until smooth. Pour into glasses and serve.

Peanuts are a good source of fibre and vitamin E for a healthy heart, and blending peanut butter with milk produces a drink that is rich in protein as well. Although peanuts contain a very high proportion of oil, this is in the form of mono- and polyunsaturated fatty acids – 'good' fats that help keep 'bad' cholesterol levels down. When buying peanut butter choose a natural brand without salt, sugar or hydrogenated oils, which are saturated fats that are often added to cheaper butters to prevent them separating.

38 peanut butter smoothie

**Makes 400 ml
(14 fl oz)**

1 banana
**2 Tbsp peanut butter,
smooth or crunchy
as preferred**
1 tsp clear honey
2 Tbsp natural yoghurt
200 ml (7 fl oz) milk
**Extra wedges of
banana, to serve**

Peel the banana and cut it into three or four pieces. Place in a liquidizer with the peanut butter, honey and yoghurt, and whiz until smooth. Add the milk and blend again until it is evenly mixed in. Pour into glasses and serve decorated with an extra wedge of banana.

Made with some of children's favourite fruits – watermelon, red grapes and sweet, fragrant strawberries – you can give this drink a fun final flourish by tucking a slice of dragon fruit over the side of the glass. Looking like a miniature hot-pink (or sometimes sunshine-yellow) rugby ball, dragon fruit have scaly skins and, depending on which variety is in season, creamy-white or vivid purple-red flesh dotted with tiny black seeds. As the drink separates quite quickly on standing, serve it with a long spoon or straw to stir it up.

40   red dragon

Makes 700 ml (1¼ pt)

350 g (12½ oz) wedge of watermelon

75 g (2½ oz) seedless red grapes

115 g (4 oz) strawberries

300 ml (½ pt) apple juice

Wedges of dragon fruit, to serve (optional)

Peel the watermelon and discard the seeds. Cut the flesh into chunks. Remove the grapes from the stalk and hull the strawberries, cutting any large ones into halves or quarters. Put the watermelon, grapes, strawberries and apple juice in a liquidizer and blend until smooth. Skim off any excess froth if preferred and pour into glasses. Serve with wedges of dragon fruit.

Blackcurrants are rich in vitamin C – just 28 g (1 oz) providing 60 mg of this important vitamin. However, their tart, almost musky flavour isn't terribly popular with children so to overcome this without adding lots of sugar, disguise the sharpness of the blackcurrants by blitzing them with creamy yoghurt and sweet cantaloupe melon. If the kids still complain the drink is too sour, a drizzle of clear honey added to the liquidizer with the fruit should have them smiling again.

42 on-your-marks smoothie

Makes 700 ml (1¼ pt)

75 g (2½ oz) blackcurrants

½ cantaloupe melon

150 ml (¼ pt) pineapple juice

200 g (7 oz) natural yoghurt

Extra sticks of melon, to serve

Pull the blackcurrants off their stalks. Peel the melon, discard the seeds and chop the flesh into chunks. Put the blackcurrants, melon, pineapple juice and yoghurt into a liquidizer and blend until smooth. Pour into glasses and serve with a couple of melon sticks in each.

Although blackberries are now widely cultivated, no punnet bought from a supermarket can match the flavour of the wild blackberries you and your children gather from country hedgerows or the fun you'll have collecting them. Blackberries are rich in vitamins C and E, which help keep the heart and circulation healthy and fight infections – plus they're also a good source of fibre.

44 true blue smoothie

Makes 600 ml (1 pt)

175 g (6 oz)
blackberries

115 g (4 oz)
blueberries

200 ml (7 fl oz)
orange juice

150 g (5½ oz)
natural yoghurt

Orange slices and
extra blueberries,
to serve

Hull the blackberries, if necessary, and remove any stalks from the blueberries. Put both in a liquidizer and add the orange juice and yoghurt. Blitz until smooth and pour into glasses. Serve with orange slices and extra blueberries.

When we think of good sources of vitamin C most of us put oranges top of our list. However, weight for weight, kiwi fruit contain more of the valuable vitamin than oranges, and just one of these small, hairy, nutritional powerhouses will provide 100% of a child's recommended daily allowance of vitamin C. The drink will thicken on standing so let it down to the desired consistency with water or extra orange juice, if necessary.

46

kiwi, orange and melon buzz

Makes 700 ml (1¼ pt)

1 kiwi fruit

400 g (14 oz) wedge of honeydew melon

300 ml (½ pt) orange juice

Peel the kiwi fruit and chop it into chunks. Peel the melon wedge and discard the seeds. Put the kiwi fruit, melon and orange juice into a liquidizer and blend until smooth. Pour into glasses and serve.

Although grapefruit are naturally sharp, the deeper their colour, the sweeter they taste, so pink or ruby fruit are likely to be more popular with children than pale yellow-fleshed ones. Red fruit will also give this juice eye appeal, tinting it with a pretty rosy-orange glow that kids will love. Like all citrus fruits, grapefruit are an excellent source of vitamin C, half a grapefruit containing around 45 mg.

grapefruit, orange and apple medley

**Makes 400 ml
(14 fl oz)**

1 grapefruit,
preferably pink or ruby

1 large orange

150 ml (¼ pt)
apple juice

Cut the rind and pith away from the grapefruit and orange and divide the flesh into segments. Place the flesh in a liquidizer, add the apple juice and blitz until smooth. Skim or drain off excess froth if preferred before pouring into glasses and serving.

48 mid-morning snacks

Folate is essential for maintaining healthy blood cells, the nervous system and helping prevent anaemia but getting your kids to eat leafy green vegetables, a rich source of folate, can be an uphill struggle. As folate can also be lost during cooking, adding fresh spinach leaves to a smoothie is a great way of preserving their nutrients and also persuading your little ones that 'green is good'.

50 cool green giant

**Makes 500 ml
(18 fl oz)**

150 g (5½ oz)
seedless green grapes

50 g (2 oz) young
spinach leaves

¼ cucumber

300 ml (½ pt)
apple juice

Cucumber sticks,
to serve

Pull the grapes off their stalks and place in a liquidizer. Remove any tough stalks from the spinach and shred the leaves coarsely. Peel and deseed the cucumber, and add both to the liquidizer with the apple juice. Blend until smooth, stopping once or twice to push down any leaves that stick to the sides. Pour into glasses and serve garnished with sticks of cucumber.

If you have a juice extractor you can make your own carrot juice, otherwise buy it ready-made. Carrots make an excellent addition to kids' drinks as not only do they add natural sweetness to tempt young palates, they are a true superfood hero with one large carrot containing enough beta-carotene to supply a whole day's allowance of vitamin A.

52 orange glow

Makes 600 ml (1 pt)

1 pear

1 large orange

300 ml (½ pt) carrot juice

Orange wedges, to serve

Peel, core and chop the pear. Cut the peel and pith away from the orange and divide the fruit into segments. Place the pear, orange and carrot juice in a liquidizer and blend until smooth. Pour into glasses and serve with orange wedges.

Look for Alfonso mangoes when they are in season during April and May as these medium-sized fruits from India have the most intense flavour and deepest orange flesh of the 2,500 plus varieties of mango that grow in tropical climes around the world. Yellow-skinned rather than green, they are delicious eaten raw or made into a long cool drink. If Alfonso mangoes are unavailable, any type of mango could be used – the riper and sweeter, the better.

54 mango, peach and apricot sparkle

**Makes 850 ml
(1 pt 9 fl oz)**

1 medium mango

1 yellow-fleshed
peach

2 fresh apricots or
4 apricot halves
canned in juice

500 ml (18 fl oz)
sparkling water

Peel the mango and cut the flesh away from the fibrous centre stone. Put the peach and fresh apricots, if using, in a heatproof bowl, pour over boiling water to cover and leave for 1 minute. Drain and cool under cold water. Cut the fruit in halves or quarters, remove the stones and peel away the skin. Put the mango, peach and apricot flesh in a liquidizer, add 150 ml (¼ pt) of the water and blend until smooth. Pour the fruit purée into glasses to half fill and top up with the rest of the water. Serve at once.

Galia and Ogen melons are closely related, the only difference being their skin. A Galia melon has a tough, dry skin that looks as though a coarse grey-green net has been stretched over it, whilst an Ogen's skin is smooth and soft, and similar in texture to that of a watermelon. When ripe, both melons are equally fragrant and juicy but, although they provide some vitamin A and C, their main contribution to a drink is to add a natural sweetness. The yoghurt gives this juice quite a tart flavour so if it's not to younger children's taste, add a teaspoon of honey.

nectarine, melon and yoghurt refresher

Makes 600 ml (1 pt)

1 nectarine
200 g (7 oz) wedge of Galia or Ogen melon
200 g (7 oz) natural yoghurt
150 ml (¼ pt) pineapple juice

Put the nectarine in a heatproof bowl, pour over boiling water to cover and leave for 1 minute. Drain, cool the nectarine under cold water and cut into quarters. Remove the stone and peel off the skin. Discard the seeds from the melon and cut away the peel. Chop the flesh into chunks. Place the nectarine, melon and yoghurt in a liquidizer and add the pineapple juice. Blitz until smooth, then pour into glasses and serve.

Bananas are invaluable when making drinks for kids as they are highly nutritious and children love their sweet flavour. They also thicken a drink so make excellent smoothies where all the fruit is blended together. As bananas contain no juice, they can't be put through a juicing machine so if you use a juicer to make drinks, blend the banana in a food processor or liquidizer separately with the milk and stir it into the drink at the end.

58   dream team

Makes 700 ml (1¼ pt)

2 tangerines
1 small banana
115 g (4 oz) blackcurrants
300 ml (½ pt) milk
Kiwi fruit slices, to serve

Peel the tangerines and pull off any loose pith. Peel the banana and cut into three or four pieces. Remove the blackcurrants from their stalks. Put the tangerines, banana and blackcurrants into a liquidizer, add the milk and blend until smooth. Pour into glasses and serve garnished with slices of kiwi fruit.

Many different varieties of pear are available but the best ones for making kids' drinks are those with yellow skins and fragrant, melting flesh, such as Williams or Comice, as they will add a natural sweetness. When pears are puréed in a liquidizer or put through a juice machine they produce a lot of froth, even when mixed with other fruit, so skim this off or serve the drink with a straw.

60   jolly red reviver

Makes 800 ml (1 pt 8 fl oz)

1 large pear

115 g (4 oz) strawberries

115 g (4 oz) red cherries, fresh or canned in fruit juice (drained weight)

350 ml (12 fl oz) cranberry juice

Cut the pear into quarters, remove the stalk and core. Peel away the skin and put the flesh in a liquidizer. Hull the strawberries, cut any large ones into halves or quarters. If using fresh cherries, pull them off their stalks and remove the stones. Add to the liquidizer with the strawberries and cranberry juice and blend until smooth. Pour into glasses and serve.

The natural sweetness of clementines and carrots will make this juice popular with children of all ages and if you pop a few carrot sticks into each glass as a garnish, you'll up their daily intake of beta-carotene too. Small baby carrots look pretty, taste sweeter and have more kid-appeal but it's the deeper-orange, main crop carrots that contain more of the healthy nutrient.

62 tomato, carrot and clementine bliss

Makes 700 ml (1¼ pt)

250 g (9 oz) tomatoes
1 stick of celery
2 clementines
300 ml (½ pt) carrot juice
Carrot and celery sticks, to serve

Put the tomatoes in a heatproof bowl, pour over boiling water to cover and leave to stand for 30 seconds. Drain and cool the tomatoes under cold water. Cut into quarters, scoop out the seeds and discard, and peel off the skins. Pull off any coarse strings from the celery and chop into 5 cm (2 in) pieces. Peel the clementines and pull away any loose pith. Place the tomato flesh, celery, clementines and carrot juice in a liquidizer and blend until smooth. Pour into glasses and add a few long, thin carrot and celery sticks to each serving as stirrers as the juice separates quite quickly on standing.

This drink can be made using either fresh or frozen raspberries. If using fresh and you want a chilled drink, add a few ice cubes to the liquidizer with the fruit; if using frozen, omit the ice cubes and blitz the berries with the banana, grapes and milk without defrosting them first. If your kids complain about the pips, substitute blueberries or strawberries for the raspberries.

64 raspberry and grape breeze

Makes 1 litre (1¾ pt)

115 g (4 oz) seedless red or green grapes

1 small banana

6 ice cubes (if using fresh berries)

175 g (6 oz) raspberries, fresh or frozen

600 ml (1 pt) milk

Extra raspberries, to serve

Pull the grapes off their stalks, peel the banana and cut it into three or four pieces. If using fresh raspberries, add the ice cubes to a liquidizer and whizz until slushy; if using frozen raspberries, omit the ice cubes. Add the grapes, banana, raspberries and milk, and blend until smooth and frothy. Pour into glasses and drop in a few extra raspberries. Serve at once.

Strawberries, like mangoes, are another fruit that kids rarely need persuading to eat as the sweet flavour of these soft, scarlet berries is very much to their taste. Packed with good things such as high levels of vitamin C – 100 g (3½ oz) strawberries provides almost twice the recommended daily allowance – soluble fibre and iron, they are excellent puréed in a fruit drink, adding colour, texture and a natural sweetness. If using a food processor, the fruit can be puréed on its own without the addition of the orange juice.

long, tall cooler

Makes 1 litre (1¾ pt)

¼ papaya, weighing about 150 g (5½ oz)

200 g (7 oz) wedge honeydew melon

115 g (4 oz) strawberries

600 ml (1 pt) orange juice

Ice cubes

Peel and remove the seeds from the papaya and melon. Hull the strawberries and cut any large ones into halves or quarters. Put the papaya, melon and strawberries into a liquidizer with 150 ml (¼ pt) of the orange juice and blend until smooth. Add a few ice cubes to tall glasses, spoon in the fruit purée and top up with the remaining orange juice. Add a stirrer or straw to each glass so kids can mix the fruit purée with the orange juice before drinking.

Apples vary in skin colour from bright green, yellow and orange to deep red and russet-brown with many variations in between and their flesh can be white, yellow or pink. Any dessert apple is suitable for this recipe, as even the sharper-flavoured varieties like Granny Smith, Egremont Russet or Braeburn will produce an attractively sweet drink. Threading a few extra blueberries and strawberries on to a cocktail stick and balancing it across the top of the glass adds a sophisticated flourish kids will appreciate.

66   juicy lucy

**Makes 800 ml
(1 pt 8 fl oz)**

1 apple

**115 g (4 oz)
blueberries**

**115 g (4 oz)
strawberries**

**300 ml (½ pt)
orange juice**

**Extra blueberries and
strawberries, to serve**

Twist the stalk off the apple, cut it into quarters, and remove the core and skin. Pull any stalks off the blueberries and hull the strawberries, halving or quartering any that are large. Put the apple, blueberries, strawberries and orange juice in a liquidizer and blend until smooth. Pour into glasses and decorate each with a few extra blueberries and strawberries.

For centuries, Native American medicine relied on cranberry juice to relieve the misery of cystitis and bladder infections and now modern science has proved that one glass of the ruby-hued nectar is ten times more effective than a course of antibiotics. Originally it was believed the juice's acidity killed off bugs but it has now been shown that its effectiveness comes from substances contained in the cranberries that stick to the walls of the urinary tract and reduce the ability of bacteria to multiply and cause infection.

68 orange and cranberry boost

Makes 700 ml (1¼ pt)

1 large orange

1 apple

300 ml (½ pt) cranberry juice

150 ml (¼ pt) white grape juice

Cut the peel and pith away from the orange and divide the flesh into segments. Twist the stalk off the apple, cut it into quarters, and remove the core and skin. Put the orange, apple, cranberry and white grape juices in a liquidizer and blend until smooth. Skim off any excess froth, if preferred, before pouring into glasses.

Mangoes contain substantial amounts of vitamins A and C, fibre, potassium and iron, plus they're packed with powerful antioxidants, all of which is good news for mums and dads, but it is their incomparable taste that will most impress the kids. Probably the most popular and widely eaten of all tropical fruits, mangoes are native to India, with a history going back over four millennia, but they are now grown around the world in Australia, Africa, Latin America and the Caribbean, ensuring a regular supply can be shipped to cooler climes for most of the year.

70 sunseeker

Makes 900 ml (1½ pt)

1 medium mango
1 small banana
1 kiwi fruit
150 ml (¼ pt) orange juice
300 ml (½ pt) milk
Kiwi fruit slices, to serve

Peel the mango and cut the flesh away from the fibrous centre stone. Peel the banana and cut it into three or four pieces. Peel the kiwi fruit. Put the mango flesh, banana and kiwi fruit in a liquidizer, and add the orange juice and milk. Process until smooth, then pour into glasses and serve with kiwi slices tucked over the side.

The 'blush' in this drink comes from strawberries and this makes a lovely summer drink when the soft berries are at their plumpest and most fragrant. If rambutans are not available, lychees could be used instead as the fruits are closely related and taste much the same, although rambutans are slightly less acidic. Native to the Malay Peninsula, rambutans differ from lychees in that they have a soft rind covered in dense red hairs, their name deriving from the Malaysian word 'rambut', meaning hair.

72 rambutan blush

Makes 700 ml (1¼ pt)

8 rambutans

175 g (6 oz) strawberries

150 ml (¼ pt) pineapple juice

150 ml (¼ pt) orange juice

Peel the rambutans and remove the stones. Hull the strawberries, cutting any large ones into halves or quarters. Place the rambutans and strawberries in a liquidizer and add the pineapple and orange juices. Blitz until smooth, then pour into glasses and serve at once.

Native to southern Mexico and Costa Rica, it was the Spaniards who took the papaya to Manila in the 16th century, from where the fruit's popularity spread around the world. This migration resulted in fruits of wildly varying shape and size, from small, yellow pears to long, green giants that weigh several kilos and are the size of vegetable marrows. Whatever their shape, inside papayas are always the same, packed with shiny black, round seeds and orange flesh that is a rich source of vitamins A and C and calcium. Cape gooseberries are also known by their Latin name of physalis.

74 going for gold

Makes 700 ml (1¼ pt)

200 g (7 oz) papaya (about half a small fruit)

1 yellow-fleshed peach

4 Cape gooseberries

300 ml (½ pt) carrot juice

150 ml (¼ pt) apple juice

Extra Cape gooseberries, to serve

Scoop the seeds out of the papaya using a spoon, peel off the skin and chop the flesh into chunks. Put the peach in a heatproof bowl, pour over boiling water to cover and leave for 1 minute. Drain, cool under cold water, then cut the peach into quarters, discarding the stone and the skin. Remove the Cape gooseberries from their papery wrapping. Put the papaya, peach, Cape gooseberries, carrot and apple juices in a liquidizer, and blend until smooth. Pour into glasses, decorate each with a Cape gooseberry and serve at once.

Not many kids can be persuaded to eat beetroot as a vegetable but blending it with some naturally sweet fruit like apples or pears to disguise its earthy flavour, makes a beautiful jewel-coloured juice they'll love. Beetroot is packed with minerals and vitamins that help cleanse the blood and keep kids going through the day so gives any drink a big healthy boost.

76   red planet

**Makes 800 ml
(1 pt 8 fl oz)**

125 g (4½ oz)
cooked beetroot

1 apple

1 tangerine

300 ml (½ pt)
cranberry juice

115 g (4 oz)
natural yoghurt

Apple wedges,
to serve

Peel the beetroot and cut into small pieces. Twist the stalk off the apple, cut it into quarters, then peel and remove the core. Peel the tangerine and pull away any loose pith. Cut in half across the middle and discard any pips. Put the beetroot, apple, tangerine and cranberry juice in a liquidizer and blend until smooth. Add the yoghurt and whizz again briefly until combined. Pour into glasses and serve at once with apple wedges.

Native to Jamaica but also grown in the US, no one is quite sure exactly what an ugli fruit is. Some say it's a cross between a mandarin and an orange, others cite tangerine and grapefruit, whilst still more suggest pomelo and bitter orange. Whatever the verdict, everyone agrees the ugli is delicious to eat, its orange-pink flesh being sweeter than that of grapefruit and therefore more appealing to children. Teamed with pear and orange, it makes a very refreshing juice.

78　ugli, orange and pear buzz

Makes 700 ml (1¼ pt)

1 ugli

1 pear

300 ml (½ pt) orange juice

150 ml (¼ pt) still mineral water

Pear wedges, to serve

Peel the ugli, removing the pith as well, and divide the flesh into segments. Twist the stalk off the pear, cut it in quarters and remove the core and peel. Put the ugli, pear, orange juice and mineral water in a liquidizer and blend until smooth. Pour into glasses and serve at once with pear wedges.

80   **afternoon treats and party time**

Watermelons were grown 5,000 years ago by the ancient Egyptians, and their sweet, crunchy flesh is still as popular today. Mark Twain said that *'when one has tasted watermelon he knows what the angels eat'* and few thirsty drinkers, whatever their age, would disagree when trying this long, cooling juice. Watermelon's deep-red flesh contains powerful antioxidants and concentrated amounts of vitamins A and C so, as well as tasting delicious, it is packed with good things too.

82   two melon treat

Makes 700 ml (1¼ pt)

700 g (1½ lb) watermelon (a good-sized wedge or about half a mini one)

150 g (5½ oz) wedge of honeydew melon

150 ml (¼ pt) apple juice

1 Tbsp lemon juice

Peel the watermelon and honeydew melon, remove the seeds and cut the flesh into chunks. Put the flesh of both melons into a liquidizer, add the apple and lemon juices and blend thoroughly until smooth. Pour into a jug and chill well before serving in tall glasses with or without ice.

Grenadine will brighten up any party drink and give it a grown-up feel that kids will love. A non-alcoholic syrup made from pomegranate juice, only the merest splash is needed to produce a vivid red-pink hue. Grenadine also adds a touch of sweetness and if it is added to a glass after the juice has been poured in, it will sink to the bottom and create an eye-catching sunrise or sunset effect.

84 sundowner

Makes 600 ml (1 pt)

2 peaches, white- or yellow-fleshed

300 ml (½ pt) orange juice

150 ml (¼ pt) pineapple juice

Splash of grenadine, to serve

Put the peaches in a heatproof bowl and pour over boiling water to cover. Leave for 1 minute before draining and cooling under cold water. Cut the peaches into quarters, remove the stones and peel away the skin. Put the peaches in a liquidizer and add the orange and pineapple juices. Blitz until smooth and pour into glasses. Add a small splash of grenadine to each glass and serve as soon as the grenadine has had time to settle at the bottom.

Lychees are a naturally sweet fruit, making them popular with children, plus they're a good source of vitamin C, containing more than either oranges or lemons. They also have as much fibre as an apple with its skin on and plenty of potassium for building cells and nerves and ensuring that blood pressure stays at a healthy level. As lychees are generally canned in syrup, it's best to buy fresh ones when they're in season and freeze some for future use. Pack unpeeled fruit in sealed plastic bags and remove the skins and stones when needed.

86 jungle fever

Makes 700 ml (1¼ pt)

2 pineapple rings, fresh or canned in fruit juice

8 lychees

150 ml (¼ pt) thick coconut milk

300 ml (½ pt) milk

Crushed ice, to serve

A little ground cinnamon or finely grated nutmeg (optional)

If using fresh pineapple, cut away the skin, dig out the brown 'eyes' with the point of a sharp knife and remove the tough centre core. Cut the flesh into chunks and place in a liquidizer. Peel the lychees and remove the stones. Add to the liquidizer with the coconut milk and milk, and blend until smooth and creamy. Add crushed ice to glasses and pour in the drink. Serve sprinkled with a little ground cinnamon or finely grated nutmeg, if liked.

After carol singing on a cold December night, a warming glass of this fruit cup will get the whole family into the Christmas spirit. If you're planning a festive party for the kids, increase the quantities of ingredients according to the numbers invited and serve the cup warm in a punch bowl with lots of extra fruit floated on top. The cup can also be served cold. Leave it to cool completely before removing the cinnamon and ginger and ladling into a punch bowl.

88 christmas party cup

Makes 700 ml (1¼ pt)

1 apple

1 large orange

2 pineapple rings, fresh or canned

300 ml (½ pt) clementine juice

300 ml (½ pt) cranberry juice

1 cinnamon stick

1 cm (½ in) piece of root ginger

Clementine and apple slices, to serve

Twist the stalk off the apple, cut into quarters, and remove the core and peel. Cut away the peel and pith from the orange, remove any pips and divide the flesh into segments. Cut the pineapple rings into chunks. Put the apple, orange and pineapple into a liquidizer and add the clementine juice. Blend until smooth and pour into a saucepan. Stir in the cranberry juice and add the cinnamon stick. Peel the ginger, slice and add to the pan. Heat gently until simmering. Lift out the cinnamon and ginger and spoon into heatproof glasses. Float clementine and apple slices on top and serve.

The ice cream turns this into an occasional treat rather than an everyday drink, although the slow-release energy provided by bananas, plus the calcium and other nutrients that are packed into milk, help to raise its healthy credentials and keep junior hunger pangs at bay until teatime. Serve the shake in tall glasses with a straw and a long spoon to scoop up the very last drops of ice cream from the bottom.

90

chocolate, coconut and banana shake

Makes 800 ml (1 pt 8 fl oz)

4 Tbsp thick coconut milk

450 ml (¾ pt) milk

1 banana

4 scoops of good-quality chocolate ice cream

Put the coconut milk and milk in a liquidizer. Peel the banana and cut it into three or four pieces. Add it to the liquidizer and blend until smooth. Add the ice cream and blend again briefly until the mixture is smooth but the ice cream hasn't completely melted. Pour into sundae glasses and serve at once with straws and long spoons.

A refreshing long drink with a tropical flavour and pretty orange-pink hue that would be fun to serve for a Caribbean or South Sea Island themed party. Serve with a stirrer or straw so the frozen papaya purée can be mixed with the sparkling water before drinking. As an alternative to papaya, try making the drink using a 350 g (12½ oz) wedge of watermelon. The mineral water could also be replaced with sparkling apple juice.

92   papaya frappé

Makes 1 litre (1¾ pt)

1 medium papaya, weighing about 350 g (12½ oz)

4 Tbsp crushed ice

175 ml (6 fl oz) orange juice

600 ml (1 pt) sparkling mineral or soda water

Halve the papaya and scoop out the seeds. Peel and chop the flesh into chunks. Put the papaya flesh, crushed ice and orange juice into a liquidizer and blend until smooth. Pour into tall glasses to roughly half fill and carefully top up with the sparkling water. Serve with a stirrer or straw in each glass and stir before drinking.

Sweet, juicy raspberries are a real taste of summer and in this drink they are teamed with peaches, another luscious sunshine fruit. As well as having a delicious flavour that kids love, raspberries are also a healthy treat containing sizeable amounts of iron, vitamin C, fibre and flavonoids that are potent antioxidants. After simmering the raspberries, sieve them to remove the pips or leave the pips in as preferred.

94 disco melba ripple

Makes 700 ml (1¼ pt)

350 g (12½ oz) raspberries

200 ml (7 fl oz) apple juice

2 peaches

300 g (10½ oz) natural yoghurt

Put the raspberries and 2 tablespoons of the apple juice in a pan and simmer gently until pulpy, mashing occasionally with a spoon. Allow to cool and then sieve to remove the seeds. Put the peaches in a heatproof bowl, pour over boiling water to cover and leave for 1 minute. Drain and cool under cold water. Cut into quarters, remove the stones and pull off the skins. Add the peaches to a liquidizer with the rest of the apple juice and the yoghurt, and whiz until smooth. Divide the raspberry purée between glasses and pour in the yoghurt mixture. Drag it through the yoghurt using a lolly stick to create a rippled effect.

Perfect for Hallowe'en or a Harry Potter themed party. If you own a heavy-duty juice machine, you can make the 'brew' even more authentic by substituting homemade pumpkin juice for the carrot. To make pumpkin juice, cut the peeled, seeded pumpkin flesh into small pieces, or it will be difficult to push through the machine, and juice it along with the oranges that should be peeled but have their pith left on.

96   witches' brew

**Makes 800 ml
(1 pt 8 fl oz)**

2 large oranges

**2 pineapple rings,
fresh or canned in juice**

**600 ml (1 pt) carrot or
pumpkin juice**

Cut the peel and pith away from the oranges and remove any pips. Divide the flesh into segments. Chop the pineapple and place in a liquidizer with the orange segments. Add the carrot or pumpkin juice and blend until smooth. Pour into glasses and serve at once with spooky black straws.

A great party drink for older children who will enjoy this fruity sparkler. An alcohol-free version of the famous Buck's Fizz champagne and orange juice cocktail, serve the drink in tall, slim flutes and add a colourful fruit garnish such as a strawberry, raspberry, kiwi fruit slice or wedge of orange, dropping the fruit into the drink or tucking it over the side of each glass. For a pretty pink variation, replace either the apple or the orange juice with cranberry juice.

98 buck's fizz mocktail

Makes 1.1 litres (2 pt)

300 ml (½ pt) apple juice

300 ml (½ pt) orange juice

600 ml (1 pt) chilled sparkling water

Fresh fruit, to serve

Pour enough apple juice into each glass to fill by one quarter. Add the same amount of orange juice and top up with chilled sparkling water. Decorate each drink with a small piece of fresh fruit.

A long, cooling summertime drink that is just right for a barbecue or picnic in the back garden or at the beach. To transport the drink, measure all the ingredients, including the ice, into a thermos flask and shake well before pouring into glasses. The drink can be made with other juices instead of grapefruit – orange, pineapple and carrot would all work well – just amend the name to suit the colour!

100   pink cloud

Makes 700 ml (1¼ pt)

1 pear or apple
350 ml (12 fl oz) pink or ruby grapefruit juice
300 ml (½ pt) cranberry juice
Pear or apple wedges, to serve

Twist the stalk off the pear or apple, cut into quarters, peel and remove the core. Pour the grapefruit juice into a liquidizer, add the pear or apple pieces along with the cranberry juice, and blend until smooth. Skim off any excess froth, if preferred, then pour into glasses and serve with wedges of pear or apple.

Served in fancy cocktail glasses with the top edge of each glass dusted with finely grated chocolate, this drink should prove a hit with young teens desperate to look grown up. Other brightly coloured fruits such as strawberries, kiwi, raspberries or papaya could be used instead of mango. If serving with strawberries, dust the rim of the glasses with white rather than dark chocolate.

102   mango crush

Makes 900 ml (1½ pt)

1 orange

50 g (2 oz) finely grated dark chocolate

2 small or 1 large mango

400 ml (14 fl oz) apple juice

Mango slices, to serve

Cut a small wedge from the orange and rub it around the rim of each glass. Spread out the grated chocolate on a plate and dip the rims of the glasses in the chocolate until coated in an even layer. Peel the mangoes and cut the flesh away from the fibrous centre stone. Put the mango in a liquidizer with the apple juice and squeeze in the juice from the rest of the orange. Blend until smooth, pour into glasses and serve at once with small mango slices.

Although pineapple contains only half as much vitamin C as citrus fruits and lower levels of vitamin A than papaya or mango, it does provide a useful amount of dietary fibre, and its sweet-sour flavour complements other fruits well in a juice or smoothie. This refreshing combination of red grapes, pear and pineapple juice served over ice should prove a hit with older children.

104   tip of the iceberg

Makes 1 litre (1¾ pt)

175 g (6 oz) seedless
red grapes

2 pears

500 ml (18 fl oz)
pineapple juice

Ice cubes or
crushed ice

Melon slices, to serve
(optional)

Pull the grapes off their stalks and place in a liquidizer. Twist the stalks off the pears, cut the fruit into quarters and remove the cores and skins. Add the pear quarters to the liquidizer with the pineapple juice and blend until smooth. Half fill glasses with ice cubes or crushed ice, then pour in the drink and serve. As the juice separates quite quickly, add a slice of melon or a straw to each glass so the contents can be given a good stir before drinking.

Rich and creamy, this smoothie will taste naturally sweet and honeyed if made with ripe fresh apricots when they are in season and at their best. Apricot halves canned in fruit juice would also work well and the drink could be diluted with some of the juice from the can if it is too thick. Instead of apricots, the drink could be made with either two peaches or two nectarines.

106   creamy apricot delight

Makes 600 ml (1 pt)

4 apricots
1 small banana
100 ml (3½ fl oz) orange juice
150 g (5½ oz) natural yoghurt
150 ml (¼ pt) milk
Extra apricot wedges and orange slices, to serve

Put the apricots in a heatproof bowl and pour over boiling water to cover. Leave for 1 minute, then drain and cool under cold water. Cut the apricots in half, remove the stones and peel off the skins. The apricots can be left unpeeled, if preferred. Peel the banana and cut into three or four pieces. Put the apricots and banana in a liquidizer, add the orange juice and blend until smooth. Add the yoghurt and milk and blend again until evenly mixed. Pour into glasses and serve at once, decorating each glass with a small apricot wedge and an orange slice.

Another great party drink for a summer get-together for older children when soft fruits are at their best. The drink can be enjoyed all year round, however, as raspberries freeze well and although strawberries lose their texture when frozen, it's not a problem as they retain all their flavour and are puréed for this drink. Try making the lemonade using blackberries instead of raspberries, or a mix of fruits of the forest berries.

108 red berry lemonade

Makes 1 litre (1¾ pt)

225 g (8 oz) strawberries

225 g (8 oz) raspberries

2 Tbsp clear honey

Finely grated zest and juice of 1 lemon

750 ml (1 pt 7 fl oz) sparkling mineral or soda water

Ice cubes

Extra raspberries and strawberries, to serve

Hull the strawberries and cut any large ones into halves or quarters. Put the strawberries and raspberries in a pan, add the honey, and heat gently until the fruit is soft and the honey has melted, mashing the fruit occasionally with a wooden spoon. Push the fruit through a sieve to remove the seeds and spoon the purée into a large jug – you should have about 225 ml (8 fl oz) of purée. Stir in the finely grated zest and juice of the lemon. Top up with the sparkling water and stir well. Half fill glasses with ice cubes and pour in the drink. Decorate with extra raspberries and strawberries.

With their soft, orange flesh and musky scent, cantaloupe melons are deliciously sweet and make perfect additions to juices. Known as rock melon in Australia, the cantaloupe belongs to the same family as cucumber, squash and pumpkin and makes a valuable contribution to our recommended daily intake of vitamins A and C, and potassium. When buying, choose the ripest melon you can find as the riper it is, the more antioxidants it will have.

grape expectations

**Makes 800 ml
(1 pt 8 fl oz)**

175 g (6 oz) seedless
green grapes

¼ cantaloupe melon

400 ml (14 fl oz)
orange juice

Extra grapes, to serve

Pull the grapes off their stalks. Peel the melon, scoop out the seeds and cut the flesh into chunks. Put the grapes and melon in a liquidizer, add the orange juice and blend until smooth. Pour into glasses and serve decorated with extra grapes.

Unsweetened coconut milk is available in cartons and cans but you can make your own too. To do this, grate fresh coconut flesh into a measuring jug and stir in an equal amount of hot, but not boiling, water. Leave to stand for 30 minutes, then place a piece of muslin over a bowl (or use a very fine sieve) and strain the coconut through it, pressing down firmly with a wooden spoon to extract as much liquid as possible. If grated coconut is put in a measuring jug up to the 300 ml (½ pt) mark and the same amount of water added, the quantity of milk produced should be about 300 ml (½ pt).

112   pink coconut bonanza

Makes 700 ml (1¼ pt)

175 g (6 oz) strawberries

1 nectarine

150 ml (¼ pt) coconut milk

175 ml (6 fl oz) pineapple juice

Crushed ice and extra strawberries, to serve

Hull the strawberries and cut any large ones into halves or quarters. Put the nectarine in a heatproof bowl, pour over boiling water to cover and set aside for 1 minute. Drain, cool the nectarine under cold water, then cut into quarters. Remove the stone and peel off the skin. Put the strawberries, nectarine, coconut milk and pineapple juice into a liquidizer, and process until smooth. Half fill glasses with crushed ice and pour in the drink. Serve with extra strawberries.

114 ice lollies, crushes and slushies

Small, sweet, seedless grapes are always popular with children, so before serving hang a small bunch of them over the side of each glass. It will make the drink more fun and also encourage kids to eat a little extra fruit. For a more vibrantly coloured drink, use red instead of green grapes and red grape juice rather than white.

116 lychee and grape slushy

Serves 4

10 lychees

115 g (4 oz) seedless green grapes

300 ml (½ pt) white grape juice

12 ice cubes

Extra small bunches of seedless green grapes, to serve

Peel the lychees and remove the stones. Pull the grapes off their stalks and place in a liquidizer with the lychees. Add the white grape juice and blend until smooth. Add half the ice cubes and blitz until the ice is broken up. Add the rest of the ice cubes and blitz again until slushy. Pour into glasses and serve decorated with small bunches of extra grapes.

Fromage frais is a fresh curd cheese made from pasteurized cow's milk. Originally from France, it is similar in taste to cottage cheese but smooth and lump free. Naturally low in fat, higher fat varieties of fromage frais are also available with added cream to give a richer flavour. If you buy small, individual tubs of fromage frais, the pots can be washed and dried, and used as lolly moulds.

118 creamy mango sticks

Serves 6 (using 50-ml/2-fl oz moulds)

1 medium mango

200 g (7 oz) natural fromage frais

2 tsp clear honey

Red fruit coulis, to serve (optional)

Peel the mango and cut the flesh away from the fibrous centre stone. Place the flesh in a liquidizer, add the fromage frais and honey, and whizz until smooth. Spoon into lolly moulds and freeze until almost firm. Push in the sticks and freeze again until solid. The lollies can be served with a red fruit coulis, such as strawberry or raspberry, as a dipping sauce, if liked.

Nectarines could be used instead of peaches and raspberries instead of strawberries if preferred. A liquidizer or food processor with a strong motor is needed to crush ice so if you're unsure how heavy-duty yours is, put the ice cubes in a plastic freezer bag and bash them with a hammer or rolling pin to break them up before blitzing with the fruit. If you try crushing ice cubes in a machine with a small motor, you risk breaking it.

120

banana, strawberry and peach slushy

Serves 6

2 peaches

2 bananas

200 g (7 oz) strawberries

150 ml (¼ pt) pineapple juice

150 ml (¼ pt) orange juice

8 ice cubes

Strawberries and peach slices, to serve

Put the peaches in a heatproof bowl and pour over boiling water to cover. Leave for 1 minute, then drain and cool under cold water. Cut into quarters, remove the stones and peel off the skins. Peel the bananas and cut into four pieces. Spread out the peach and banana on a metal tray and freeze until solid. Hull the strawberries and place in a liquidizer. Add the pineapple and orange juices and blitz until smooth. Tip in the peaches and bananas and half the ice cubes. Process for 5 seconds, add the rest of the ice cubes and blend until slushy. Spoon into glasses. Serve at once with strawberries and peach slices.

If you accidentally leave the frozen fruit in the freezer for too long and it becomes so solid you can't mash it up with a fork, remove the container from the freezer to the fridge and leave to soften a little – this will take about 15 to 20 minutes. Once softened, tip the mixture into a liquidizer or food processor and whizz until it is broken up into large crystals. Once crushed, serve immediately or the mixture will start to melt – especially on a hot day.

watermelon cooler crush

Serves 6

700 g (1 lb 9 oz) wedge of watermelon

100 g (3½ oz) strawberries

200 ml (7 fl oz) apple juice

Extra strawberries, to serve

Remove the seeds and rind from the watermelon and cut the flesh into chunks. Hull the strawberries and cut any large ones into halves or quarters. Put the watermelon, strawberries and apple juice in a liquidizer and blend until smooth. Pour into a plastic freezer container and freeze for about 2 hours, or until the mix has frozen around the edges but is still soft in the middle. Break up the frozen parts with a fork, mixing the crystals with the softer centre. Return to the freezer for another 1 hour, then fork up the mixture again. Spoon into serving dishes or glasses and serve at once, with extra strawberries.

Vividly coloured and deliciously fruity, these ice lollies taste as good as they look. If clementines are in season, use clementine juice instead of orange as kids will prefer its sweeter flavour. If you make your own fruit juices, strawberry or raspberry could replace the cranberry.

124   stop traffic lollies

Makes 8 (using 75-ml/3-fl oz moulds)

300 ml (½ pt) orange juice

300 ml (½ pt) cranberry juice

Pour the orange juice into 8 lolly moulds so they are half full. Freeze until the juice is almost solid. Push in the lolly sticks and top up with the cranberry juice. Return the lollies to the freezer for several hours until completely frozen before removing them from the moulds.

Chocolate makes these lollies a special treat and they're bound to be a hit with all ages at a birthday party. Younger children will prefer milk chocolate but for older ones use dark chocolate with a high percentage of cocoa solids as not only does plain chocolate have a stronger flavour, it's healthier too as it boosts the levels of antioxidants in the blood.

126 chocolate banana rockets

Makes 6 (using 50-ml/2-fl oz moulds)

2 bananas
150 ml (¼ pt) milk
75 ml (3 fl oz) orange juice
1 tsp clear honey
100 g (3½ oz) milk or plain chocolate

Peel the bananas and cut each one into four pieces. Place in a liquidizer, add the milk, orange juice and honey, and blend until smooth. Pour the mixture into lolly moulds so they are about three-quarters full and freeze until almost firm. Break up the chocolate into small pieces and place in a bowl over a pan of steaming, but not boiling water, without letting the bottom of the bowl touch the water. Leave until melted, stirring until smooth, then set aside to cool for a few minutes. Push sticks into the nearly frozen banana lollies and spoon the melted chocolate on top. Freeze again until solid.

Skimmed, semi-skimmed or whole cow's milk, or soya milk can be used to make these ice lollies; the higher the fat content of the milk the creamier they will be so lollies made with skimmed milk will be quite watery. Natural yoghurt or fromage frais could also be used, either to replace the milk or mixed with it in equal quantities. You could also use fruit-flavoured milk or yoghurt, but check labels for their sugar content as some can be quite high.

banana and strawberry milk lollies

Makes 8 (using 50-ml/2-fl oz moulds)

1 small banana
150 g (5½ oz) strawberries
200 ml (7 fl oz) milk

Peel the banana and cut it into three or four pieces. Hull the strawberries and cut any large ones into halves or quarters. Place the banana and strawberries in a liquidizer, add the milk and blend until smooth. Pour into lolly moulds and freeze until almost firm. Push a stick into each mould and return to the freezer until solid.

Instead of blueberries, these ice lollies could also be made with strawberries, raspberries, blackberries or another summer berry, although if using raspberries or blackberries, sieve the purée first before adding it to the moulds to remove the pips. If Greek yoghurt flavoured with honey is not available, stir 2 teaspoons of clear honey into natural Greek yoghurt.

130   blueberry yoghurt lollies

Makes 4 (using 100-ml/3½-fl oz moulds)

200 g (7 oz) blueberries
3 Tbsp apple juice
200 g (7 oz) Greek yoghurt with honey

Remove any stalks from the blueberries and place in a liquidizer. Add the apple juice and blend until smooth. Stir half the blueberry purée into the yoghurt and spoon half of this mixture into the lolly moulds. Add the rest of the blueberry purée and top with the remaining yoghurt mixture. Freeze until almost firm, then push a lolly stick into each mould and freeze again until solid.

A vivid orange treat your kids will love. Mango provides antioxidants, orange juice lots of vitamin C, and carrots are rich in carotene to ensure strong growth and healthy bodies. You can slip in some extra nutrients by topping each serving with an orange slice and a frilly curl shaved from a carrot by running a vegetable peeler down its length – get the children to see who can shave off the longest carrot curl without it breaking!

132

zingy mango, orange and carrot crush

Serves 4

1 medium mango

175 ml (6 fl oz) orange juice

50 ml (2 fl oz) carrot juice

Orange or clementine slices and carrot curls, to serve

Peel the mango and cut the flesh away from the fibrous centre stone. Put the flesh in a liquidizer, add the orange and carrot juices and blend until smooth. Pour the purée into a plastic freezer container and freeze for about 2 hours, or until frozen around the edges. Mash up the frozen part with a fork, mixing it with the softer mixture in the centre and return to the freezer for another 1 hour. Break up again with a fork. Spoon into dishes and serve decorated with orange or clementine slices and carrot curls.

Skimmed milk powder is a useful store cupboard standby that can be added straight from the pack to drinks mixes to give them a creamier consistency. It contains hardly any fat but retains all the protein, calcium and vitamins found in whole milk. It is also easier to re-constitute than whole milk powder due to its low fat levels. For an eye-catching red slushy, replace the pineapple juice with cranberry juice.

134 cherry berry slushy

Serves 4

175 g (6 oz) strawberries

175 g (6 oz) cherries

150 g (5½ oz) raspberries

300 ml (½ pt) pineapple juice

2 Tbsp dried milk powder

8 ice cubes

Extra cherries, to serve

Hull the strawberries, cutting any large fruit into halves or quarters, and stone the cherries. Put the strawberries, cherries, raspberries, pineapple juice and milk powder in a liquidizer and blend until smooth. Add half the ice cubes and blitz until they are broken up, then add the remaining ice cubes and process again until slushy. Spoon into glasses and serve decorated with extra cherries.

Like all citrus fruits, oranges are a rich source of vitamin C, plus they are high in soluble fibre and pectin, which slow down the rate at which sugar is absorbed by the body. Look for Florida oranges when they are in season as the Sunshine State's climate of hot sun followed by sudden downpours of heavy rain, produces fruit with a thinner rind and more juice than those from Spain or Jaffa.

orange salad crush

Serves 4

400 ml (14 fl oz) orange juice
1 large orange
1 kiwi fruit

Pour the orange juice into a freezer container and freeze until just solid. Cut the peel and pith away from the orange and divide the flesh into segments, discarding any pips. Peel the kiwi fruit and chop coarsely. Break up the frozen juice so it will fit into a liquidizer or food processor, then add the orange and kiwi fruit flesh and whizz until the juice is crushed and the fruit chopped. Transfer to cups or shallow dishes and serve at once.

ice lollies, crushes and slushies

When summer fruits are in season they should be sweet enough without the need for extra sugar but if your kids complain the slushy is too sharp, add a little honey to the liquidizer with the fruit. When summer fruits aren't in season, buy a pack of mixed frozen berries and blend with the apple juice whilst still solid, omitting the ice. If using a liquidizer, reduce the quantity of apple juice by half for a fruitier result.

136 summer fruit slushy

Serves 6

500 g (1 lb 2 oz) mixed summer fruits, eg strawberries, raspberries, blueberries and blackberries

20 ice cubes

300 ml (½ pt) apple juice

Extra strawberries, to serve

Prepare the fruit, removing hulls and stalks as necessary. Put half the ice cubes in a liquidizer or food processor, add the fruit and apple juice, and blitz until the ice is broken up. Add the remaining ice cubes and blend to a slush. Spoon into cups or glasses, top with extra strawberries and enjoy before the ice melts!

Belonging to the same family as peaches, nectarines, plums and cherries, apricots provide a concentrated source of vitamin C, plus beta-carotene for good eyesight and healthy skin. Ranging in colour from pale yellow to deep orange tinged with a rosy blush, apricots need warm weather to ensure they become plump, ripe and sweet. Although a deep orange colour is not always a reliable guide to flavour, very pale apricots are best avoided, along with those that have wrinkled, bruised or damaged skins.

138 pineapple and apricot crush

Serves 6

1 pineapple
6 apricots
1 banana
175 ml (6 fl oz) apple juice
100 ml (3½ fl oz) orange juice
12 ice cubes

Trim the top off the pineapple, cut away the skin and remove the brown 'eyes'. Chop into chunks, trimming away the tough centre core. If peeling the apricots, put them in a heatproof bowl, pour over boiling water to cover and leave for 1 minute. Drain and cool under cold water. Halve, remove the stones and peel off the skins. Spread out the pineapple and apricots on a tray and freeze for 1 hour, or until firm. Peel the banana, cut into four pieces and liquidize with the apple and orange juices. Add the pineapple and apricots and half the ice cubes. Blitz until the ice is crushed, add the remaining cubes and blitz again. Spoon into glasses and serve at once.

Younger children will love these tiny ice lollies that can be made using their favourite fruits – as well as cherries, strawberries, peaches, bananas and apricots all work well. They can be frozen using proper moulds if you prefer but empty fromage frais pots make lollies that are just the right size for small hands. As fruit tends to become less sweet when frozen, a little honey is added to make the lollies more appealing to young tastes.

140   cherry lolly pots

Makes 8 (using 50-ml/2-fl oz moulds)

200 g (7 oz) dark red cherries

200 g (7 oz) natural fromage frais or natural yoghurt

2 tsp clear honey

Remove the stalks and stones from the cherries and place in a liquidizer with the fromage frais or yoghurt and honey. Blend until smooth and pour into small pots. Freeze until almost firm, then push a stick into each pot and return to the freezer until solid.

142 bedtime soothers

The classic combination of chocolate and milk, topped, if the kids are good, with an extra chocolate sprinkle, should ensure that most children have a smile on their face when bedtime comes around. Use dark chocolate with a high proportion of cocoa solids rather than milk chocolate, as it has a stronger flavour, and preferably full-fat or semi-skimmed rather than skimmed milk for extra creaminess. Because this drink contains chocolate, make doubly sure they brush their teeth before bedtime!

144   real hot chocolate

Makes 350 ml (12 fl oz)

300 ml (½ pt) milk

25 g (1 oz) dark chocolate

Little extra grated chocolate, to serve

Pour the milk into a heavy saucepan. Chop the chocolate into small pieces, add to the milk and heat gently, stirring occasionally so the chocolate melts and doesn't stick to the bottom of the pan. Once the chocolate has melted, bring the milk to a gentle simmer – don't let it boil – and then remove from the heat. Pour into a mug or a heatproof glass and sprinkle with a little extra grated chocolate.

It's no myth that a glass of milk before bed helps children sleep well as milk contains trytophan, an amino acid that boosts the levels of the chemical serotonin in the brain, which is essential for helping the body relax. Bananas are another trytophan-rich food so combined with milk in a bedtime drink your kids should be guaranteed a peaceful night's sleep.

146   sweet dreams

Makes 350 ml (12 fl oz)

1 banana
75 ml (3 fl oz) pineapple juice
225 ml (8 fl oz) milk

Peel the banana and chop it into three or four pieces. Place in a liquidizer with the pineapple juice and milk and blend until smooth. Drink cold, or warm gently in a small pan and pour into a heatproof glass or mug.

Similar to caffé latte but made using cocoa powder instead of coffee to help your kids relax before bedtime at the end of a busy day. Rather than sweetening the drink with sugar, add a little honey or maple syrup or a dash of flavoured syrup such as chocolate, butterscotch or banana. If you have an espresso machine, the milk can be steamed as if you were making a cappuccino or caffé latte, otherwise simply whisk it to give it a frothy head.

148 chocco latte

Makes 300 ml (½ pt)

1 tsp cocoa powder

1 tsp honey, maple or other flavoured syrup

300 ml (½ pt) milk

Extra cocoa powder or ground cinnamon, to dust

Mix the cocoa powder and honey or syrup with a little of the milk in a tall heatproof glass or mug, stirring until the powder has dissolved. Steam the rest of the milk or put it in a small pan and slowly bring to a simmer. Remove from the heat, whisk until frothy and pour over the cocoa mixture, stirring until combined. Sprinkle with a little extra cocoa powder or ground cinnamon.

Old-fashioned lemon barley water is a childhood favourite, and it can also be made using the juice of a grapefruit or an orange in place of the lemon juice. Although cooking the barley is a lengthy process, once made, any leftover drink can be stored in the refrigerator for a week or longer. Pearl barley is barley that has had its hull and bran removed. The polishing process used to remove the bran makes the grains shiny.

150   lemon kiss

Makes 600 ml (1 pt)

75 g (2½ oz) pearl barley

2 Tbsp clear honey, or to taste

Juice of 3 large lemons

Put the pearl barley in a saucepan and add enough cold water to just cover it. Bring to the boil and then strain immediately, rinsing the barley grains under cold water. Return the barley to the pan, add 900 ml (1½ pt) water and bring to the boil. Cover the pan and simmer for 1 hour. Strain the hot liquid into a heatproof jug and discard the barley. Stir in the honey until it dissolves and leave to cool. When the barley water is cold, stir in the lemon juice. Drink cold or heat gently and serve warm.

Picking blackberries together in late summer is fun for all the family, and as the berries freeze well they can be enjoyed all year round. When sieving the plums and blackberries, press down on the pulp firmly with the back of a spoon so as much of it is pushed through the strainer as possible, and the cordial is not too thin and watery. Plums are a good source of vitamin C and any variety can be used to make this drink.

blackberry, apple and plum cordial

**Makes 800 ml
(1 pt 8 fl oz)**

225 g (8 oz) plums
350 g (12½ oz) blackberries
2 Tbsp clear honey
150 ml (¼ pt) apple juice
300 ml (½ pt) still mineral water

Cut the plums in half, remove the stones and put in a saucepan with the blackberries. Add the honey, apple juice and 150 ml (¼ pt) cold water. Simmer gently for about 10 minutes until the fruit is soft and the juices have run. Remove from the heat and leave to cool for 15 minutes. Tip the fruit and juices into a sieve set over a bowl or wide-necked jug and strain, pushing as much of the fruit pulp through the sieve as possible. You should have about 500 ml (18 fl oz). Dilute the cordial with the mineral water and serve cold or reheat until warm.

More interesting than just a glass of plain warm milk, this drink could be made using other berries such as blackberries or blueberries in place of the strawberries. It could also be served cold during the day as a milkshake with a scoop of strawberry ice cream or sorbet added for a treat.

152 strawberry and banana milk

Makes 400 ml (14 fl oz)

4 strawberries
1 small banana
350 ml (12 fl oz) milk

Hull the strawberries, cut them in half and put in a liquidizer. Peel the banana and chop it roughly. Add it to the liquidizer with the milk and blend until smooth. Transfer into a saucepan and heat gently until the milk comes to a simmer. Pour into heatproof glasses or mugs and leave until cool enough to drink.

Passion fruit eaten before going to bed are said to relax the body and encourage restful sleep. The scientific reason for this is the glycoside and flavonoid compounds they contain, so for lively kids – and their exhausted parents – this smoothie is just what the doctor ordered. The fruit are native to South America, in particular southern Brazil, where mothers ensure their hyperactive offspring stay calm by drinking a couple of glasses of passion fruit juice every day.

154 sleep tight smoothie

Makes 350 ml (12 fl oz)

3 passion fruit
1 banana
250 ml (9 fl oz) milk
1 tsp honey

Cut the passion fruit in half and scoop the pulp and seeds into a small bowl. Heat gently in the microwave until the seeds separate from the pulp. Push through a sieve set over the goblet of a liquidizer, rubbing with the back of a spoon so the pulp goes through the sieve, leaving the seeds behind. Discard the seeds. Peel the banana and cut it into three or four pieces. Add it to the liquidizer with the milk and honey and blend until smooth. Pour into glasses and serve at once.

Green tea is prized for the high level of antioxidants it contains but what's more likely to impress your kids – especially the girls – and persuade them to give it a try, is that green tea is the favourite drink of supermodels. In addition, it also aids digestion, as does the fresh mint that is used to flavour the tea in this recipe. Unlike ordinary tea, green tea is best made with water that has been boiled and left to stand for a couple of minutes as fast boiling water will spoil the flavour of the delicate leaves.

156 minty green tea

Makes 300 ml (½ pt)

1 green tea tea bag

2–3 sprigs of fresh mint

300 ml (½ pt) freshly boiled water

1 tsp clear honey or to taste (optional)

Put the tea bag and mint sprigs in a mug or heatproof glass and pour over the water. Leave to stand for 5 minutes before removing the tea bag and mint, and stirring in a little honey to taste, if desired.

A grown-up version of Polish milk and honey (see page 159), this has more sophisticated flavours that will appeal to older children. Maple syrup is useful for sweetening drinks as it has an attractive toffee flavour and contains zinc and manganese, both of which are important for a healthy immune system. Cinnamon adds a sweet spicy flavour, making the drink an ideal night cap for a cold winter's night.

158 golden slumbers

**Makes 250 ml
(9 fl oz)**

250 ml (9 fl oz) milk

**¼ tsp ground
cinnamon**

1 Tbsp maple syrup

**Few drops of vanilla
essence, or to taste**

Put the milk in a small pan and add the cinnamon and maple syrup. Warm gently until the milk comes to simmering point, then remove from the heat and add the vanilla essence. Pour into a mug or heatproof glass and serve at once.

A traditional and very simple drink from Poland that mums have relied on for generations to send their children off to the Land of Nod. When heating the milk, bring it just to simmering point so it is hot enough to melt the honey but not come to a rapid boil. A rich source of antioxidants, honey also aids digestion, making it a nutritionally better sweetener than refined sugars.

polish milk and honey

Makes 250 ml (9 fl oz)

250 ml (9 fl oz) milk

2 tsp clear honey

Put the milk and honey in a small pan and heat gently until the milk comes to a simmer, whisking or stirring occasionally so the honey dissolves. Pour into a mug or heatproof glass and serve when cool enough to drink.

160

index